When people Write with Spice, I always see three things happen: First, teachers apply this technique immediately because it is so easy to use. Next, Writing with Spice is fun, so students write more and they write well. Finally, superintendents smile more often when they learn that their writing test scores went up.

- Dr. Jay Dugan, Director of Professional/Curriculum Development EIRC

Mike's SPICE writing workshop was the best I have been to in the 16 years I have been teaching! I did not even doodle once! We were able to use what he taught us immediately and did not need to buy any expensive materials or program. I use it all the time with my basic skills students because I can adjust it to any level that I need!

- Jill L. DeRuchie, Achieve Teacher, Sabater Elementary School, Vineland, NJ

Adding "SPICE" to our writing program has improved our students' writing and our state test scores. I highly recommend implementing these strategies, and if possible, invite Mike to present them to your staff and students. His dynamic presentation motivated and excited even our most reluctant writers! The teachers loved it, too!

- Susan Grillo, Principal, Lincoln Park Elementary School, Lincoln Park, NJ

If anyone can make children love to write, it's Mike Devono! In a very organized, step by step approach, Mike models for the students his recipe for creating a writing piece that will "whet the appetites" of the readers. It is what he calls, adding "SPICE." Mike explains to the students how our food would be tasteless without spices, but when they are added the food is delicious! So, Mike "stirs the pot," and helps the students "cook-up" a writing piece filled with just the right amount of SPICE, to make the readers "hungry for more!"

- Kristine A. diCoio, Principal, E.T. Hamilton Elementary School, Voorhees, NJ

i

SPICE will move your staff to a new level of understanding and expectations while addressing the needs of NCLB in the area of Language Arts Literacy. Mike's approach and wit will enhance and enrich while being one of the most effective, beneficial and comprehensive training for teachers in a K-12 experience while exploring and reinforcing learning at a new level.

- Newlin Schoener, Director of Curriculum & Instruction,
Waterford Township Public Schools, Waterford Township, NJ

Our district state assessment scores in Language Arts Literacy have always been above the 90% mark; however a very large percentage of our students scored in the Proficient range and only a small percentage scored in the Advanced Proficient range. In an effort to increase the percentage of students who performed in the Advanced Proficient range, we brought in Mike Devono's Teaching Writing with Spice. We scheduled Mike for several sessions of professional development in each elementary school and in just one year, we were able to increase the percentage of third and fourth grade students who scored in the Advanced Proficient range on the LAL section of the New Jersey State Assessment.

- Dan Mattie, Director of Curriculum Voorhees Township Schools,
Director of Program Development, NJ

How on earth do I get my students to love writing? Well, Mike Devono's SPICE UP YOUR WRITING, of course! SPICE is "easy as 1-2-3" because it's a teacher-student friendly approach to teaching writing. My students know that "with every pair of sixes you have to end with a pair of nines" in reference to direct quotes. Mike's "SPICE advice" helped my students meet success with the NJASK: 20 out of 21 met proficiency in Language Arts Literacy with three in the advanced proficient range. As quick as a flash, SPICE will make your students' writing so enticing that it will be as enjoyable as a fresh pot of homemade tomato sauce!

- Dana E. Speziali, Petway Elementary School, Vineland, NJ

EIRC is proud to have its first published book from our Professional Development Department...and what better way to get started than to present Mike Devono's *Teaching Writing with Spice* program!

- *Dr. Charles Ivory, Executive Director, EIRC*

Printed in the United States of America

This book is printed on acid-free paper.

Cover Art: Sue V. Daly
Cover Design: Tim Litostansky
First published by Aquinas & Krone Publishing, LLC September 1, 2008
ISBN# 978-0-9800448-2-9
To schedule a teachers workshop, or a classroom visit to see "Writing with SPICE"
taught to your students by Mr. Devono, please contact:

Dr. Jay Dugan at EIRC
606 Delsea Drive
Sewell, NJ 08080
(856) 582-7000
www.eirc.com

EIRC is a public agency specializing in education-related programs and services for parents,
schools, communities, nonprofit organizations and privately held businesses throughout New
Jersey. Their programs also reach into more than 36 states and 8 foreign countries.

EIRC offers a great many resources under one roof. These range from gifted and special
education services to creative problem solving...from nationally validated programs in science,
mathematics and geography to child care and child assault prevention ... from web development,
graphics and printing to computer instruction ... and from teacher in-service and curriculum
design to international exchange programs.

Teaching Writing
with
SPICE!

THIS IS WHAT WORKS!

Teaching writing with **SPICE** - Literally

I dedicate this book to the staff of
Fairfield Primary School,
for this is where it all began.

~Mike Devono

Preface

Teaching Writing with SPICE

I designed "Teaching with SPICE" after twenty-one years teaching fourth grade. That's right – twenty-one years. Imagine being ten-years-old for over two decades and knowing year after year that the children come to you at age nine, turn ten, and leave. At the end of every school year I'd often wonder how much of my teaching skills and passion for my work would stay with these kids throughout the years. That being the case, my adult mind was always thinking of ways to improve my techniques, but, at the same time, the spirit of a child was controlling my thoughts and strategies. This was a fun combination to say the very least!

As time moved on, things changed and our teaching had to follow a curriculum set by others; however, no one told us *how* we have to teach. Teacher's manuals were okay at first, but many times I'd come to a section that gave me the perception that "this will not work with my kids"! Sometimes *I* didn't even get it. I found that after a while, I didn't need a teacher's manual. I realized that I could do a better job because I AM A TEACHER. That's what I signed up for! I felt that I could teach anything to anybody. I didn't need someone telling me that I wanted 100% of my kids to pass the test. I wanted *every* child in my class to have straight A's from day one of my teaching career!

My wheels started to spin and I immediately thought about the two things that used to give me the most trouble while teaching - problem-solving and creative writing. You are in for long days and nights on these lessons. I mean, who taught you how to write? Hmm? If you can answer that, then you're very fortunate. Most people taught themselves. What's wrong with this? Now, who taught you how to teach children how to write? Was it college? Again, most teachers taught themselves. What's wrong with this picture?

Sometimes I wonder who needs more help in education: the teachers, or the teachers who taught them how to become one. College credits are great for moving up in the education field, but what teachers really need is training that actually gives them the abilities to teach the core curriculum standards.

They need to be able to take a textbook and align it with testing strategies that are universally matched to any kind of problem-solving questions or writing test.

And so it began...

SPICE was developed over my 28½ years of teaching how to use and prepare food. I associated the spices to cooking a great-tasting soup, called "Spice Soup." Each skill or word type is a different kind of spice that gives flavor to their writing. For example, compound sentences are called **salt**; listing sentences are **pepper**; figurative language is **oregano**; and so on. Beginnings and endings are called **meat** and **potatoes** because that is how important they are. After planning our story, we would sprinkle 'spice' all over so we have varied sentence structure, a variety of words, and much more. I would tell the students I would want to 'eat' their paper with my eyes. Children seem to identify right away with food and the 'spice' needed to give it flavor.

In this book I will show you how to identify various skills needed to teach writing for all levels from grades K to College. After identifying these skills, I will show you how I taught them using proven, time-saving techniques. I will demonstrate how to apply these skills with graphic organizers and how to water it down for the lower grades. Finally, I have designed a grading system that shows your student's progression from one story to the next. It's also designed to build self-confidence. It's important to know that I feel I am *not* teaching to a test. I am teaching so far past the test that when the children take any kind of writing test, it's a piece of cake. I have actually had to teach down to some students because there were not enough pages in the test book! **SPICE** works extremely well with advanced students because it gives them a clear path of how to think while writing. It will also add to creative thinking by letting the children expand their writing, while the teacher can keep a close eye on each individual. It is almost like an individual education plan because you know who can do what. **SPICE** enables the teacher to keep track of children who have problems with self-esteem, word usage, and spelling. It is designed to adhere to all levels because you are the grader, and each child's mistakes are different.

If the teacher in grade three used **SPICE**, then the fourth grade teacher's job becomes a little easier; as does the fifth grade teacher's job, and so on. It will be a connection that is usually lost over the summer that could give you an easier start with writing. The skills stay the same, but the levels change from year to year. Constant reviewing also takes place from grade to grade because all kinds of written work require the basics. Beginnings, endings, varied sentence structure, and a variety of words are a must in all kinds of written work.

As you attempt the various techniques, keep in mind where the children are at the beginning of the year. The 'summer drain' affects all of us, and you need to set the stage in all areas, not just writing. But when you start writing, you will have a step-by-step and flexible yet rigid plan to follow. The entire staff can use it to combat the skills lost during summer vacation. **SPICE** will help students and teachers become the experienced writers who are needed to cope with the changing world of tested writing abilities - and find fun and passion for the written word in the process.

Now let's get started… and **SPICE IT UP!**

~Mike Devono

Table of Contents

I. Compositional Risks

II. Drilling and Internalizing SPICE

III. Planning for Stories, Prompts, and Essays

IV. Conferencing and Grading Papers

V. Other Prompts

VI. Timing Standards

VII. Encouragement

VIII. The Right Direction

IX. Conclusion

I. Compositional Risks

1. Descriptive Words (tenderizer)

The beginning weeks are usually dedicated to three various kinds of writing. Children in all grades need to remember run-on sentences, incomplete sentences, and what makes a good sentence. A good sentence, depending on the grade level, should be about eight to ten words for fourth through sixth grade and about five to six words for grades one and two. Having children add any kind of descriptive words helps, as it increases sentence length. A short sentence is also acceptable every now and then, because it's a varied sentence also. Usually these sentences are some kind of exclamatory sentence, e.g. "Billy, look out!", or "Do you believe him?" Please remember when teaching descriptive words to teach every synonym. Remember adjectives, adverbs, descriptive words, descriptive phrases, modifiers, and enhancing words. Questions are asked in many ways, and you need to have all loose ends covered so the students have a fair chance to succeed.

2. Compound sentences, words, subjects, and predicates (salt)

Compound sentences are an excellent way to show a simple form of a compositional risk. Second grade often has trouble with this, so we substitute compound words, subjects, predicates, and contractions. As you conference with the child, you will have to gauge each child and add in new skills when you feel they are ready. For younger children, double subjects or predicates are followed by a pronoun sentence so the child does not repeat the same words, e.g. "Bill and Pete went to the store. They went there because. . . ." Teaching this will create a two-sentence scenario in most cases.

At this time I used to introduce a unique way to insert teaching grammar into writing. I had the children say each punctuation mark whenever they needed one: "I like cake, (comma) and I like pie (period)." This actually helps the children to remember commas, periods, quotation marks, and question marks. Children, for the most part, will not proofread their work unless reminded to. Some adults have difficulty also because they wrote it; however, many people who do proofread constantly change written pieces over and over again. Children rarely do this. What you see is usually what you get. I just asked them to go through their sentences and say the punctuation. At least they're proofreading something, and they seem to get used to it.

> *I like cake, (comma) but I like pie better (period).*
> *Do you want some cake, (comma) or do you want some pie? (question mark)*
> *John said, (comma) "(sixes) I would like some cake. (period)" (nines)*
> *Frank and John went to the baseball game, (comma) boxing match, (comma) and track meet last Tuesday. (period)*

Although "(comma and)" is optional in a listing sentence, try to stay consistent at first. It's less confusing to the students, and gives them less to think about while writing.

I taught that (comma) *and,* (comma) *but,* and (comma) *or* go together like a bacon, lettuce, and tomato sandwich. Verbalizing punctuation seems to help children internalize grammar sometimes forgotten. It made my job a little easier.

3. Figurative Language (pepper)

Our lives are tied with so many various forms of figures of speech that kids don't even realize it. This concept may begin as early as second grade through watching cartoons, commercials, their parents, and even you. A good drill for this is what I used to call figurative/literal. The children literally draw a figure of speech. This internalizes the expression. Try it with "it's raining cats and dogs", or "buckets". Kids love it.

As this skill grows, the sentence does also. It needs to explain the figurative language expression, along with the essay being written.

> Here's an example:
>> *I studied all week, and the test was a piece of cake.*
>> *I understand that you want us to go to school six days a week; however, many students need their spare time because their plates are full. Please understand that spare time, to me, is like finding a needle in a haystack.*

This beginning to a persuasive essay shows how both figurative language expressions match the topic.

You decide which figurative language should and can be used while conferencing. As the children grow, so does this skill. Again, teach every synonym you can think of for figurative language expressions, e.g. similes, metaphors, descriptive phrases, idioms and idiomatic expressions, phrases that describe, and figures of speech. After the children become comfortable with figurative language, opposites can also help, e.g. "Learning how to ride my bike was <u>not</u> a piece of cake." This implies that it was not easy.

Many figurative language expressions are what I used to call "all the time" words, which means that they can be used in any kind of essay. Examples include "piece of cake", "easy as pie", "24/7", and "a walk in the park", to name a few. Lower grades can use "easy as 1, 2, 3" or "ABC". Here are some examples of "over the hill":

> *Mr. Devono is so far over the hill that he needs binoculars to see the hump anymore.*
> *Mr. Devono isn't even close to being over the hill. He beat me four out of five games.*

This enables the children to use their favorite expressions in various ways and make them more meaningful while writing. It's probably best to start out with similes. Many children relate to being as tough as a . . . , or as fast as a . . . . Remember, you're a teacher, and you're as smart as a . . . .

4. Listing Sentences (oregano)

Listing sentences are another form of compositional risk that can add flavor to a child's essay. I used to start out easy; as the child developed, so did the sentence length; for instance, "I like cake, pie, and soda," all the time saying the comma and periods. Next, I would build details into the sentence as the year progressed. A sentence now evolves to:

> *I would like to eat some delicious cake, have a nice piece of apple pie, and drink an iced mug of orange soda.*

Details not only start to make the children hungry, but they actually make the sentence spicier. Upper grades can add in details as they see fit.

> *I would love to eat some delicious chocolate-covered cake with a cherry on top, devour a warm*

slice of deep-dish apple pie, and slowly slurp
about a gallon of frosty root beer.

Using *but, and, or* in a listing sentence also creates a varied sentence.

Do you want to go to the mall, shore, or
amusement park?

Another example of using listing sentences is to put the list first, e.g. "Cake, pie, and bread are full of carbohydrates." Moving along, you can add spice to spice in situations that call for a bit more flavor.

The little boy was uptight, out of sight, but
in the groove during the game.

I call this "spice-in-spice", and this kind of sentence usually gives the reader a little chuckle.

5. Affixes (chives)

Using prefixes and suffixes can help with the perception of enhanced writing skills. Teaching what I call "all-purpose affixes" helps the child's writing flow. Some universal prefixes that can be applied to most words include *re, pro, anti, mini, super,* and suffixes: *less, like,* and *ish.* Prefixes like *un, in, im,* and *re,* to name a few, are great. Suffixes such as *er, less, ful, ly,* and *ish* also seem to flow easily in most essays. Even in the upper grades I would demonstrate the power of affixes by using a single four-letter word. For instance, I would explain that "dark" is an elementary word while "darkness" is middle school material. Adding *semi* as a prefix spices it up to "semi-darkness". Now we are using high school vocabulary by simply adding affixes. Seems easy? It is. Using affixes in opposite forms also gives a twist to writing skills.

Please do not rewrite your homework.
You are not being very careful at all.

I would try to make the students feel a prefix or suffix by telling them to rewrite every assignment completed that day. Moans and groans followed; however, the point got through to them very quickly. This actually makes a prefix tangible.

Simple verbal examples can also make a point. I'd explain that the comment, "That's not good!" is OK, but if they say, "That's totally unacceptable," or, "That is completely unsatisfactory!" it shows even more power. Using what I call "grown-up words" increases the perception of an authoritative writer.

6. Beginnings (meat)

Beginning sentences are a skill that, at first, I never even thought about until I found out that most children do not know how to start an essay. Since beginnings change from one essay to another, this skill is very confusing to younger students, and it takes about a week to teach. The level of the child determines the amount of spice in the beginning sentence as well as the complexity of this sentence. I wanted a strong beginning. If you can grab the reader from the get-go, it's a definite plus.

Teaching the importance of a good beginning was easy. I'd simply ask the children if they had ever seen a movie with a beginning that they really didn't like or understand. I know I've seen quite a few. We'd discuss the empty or confusing feeling of how a writer's beginning needs to take their audience into account. This is where I used to make sure their beginnings would reach out and grab hold of the reader. The students would start out with simple beginning words or phrases. They were simply called "beginnings" – for example:

"Many years ago," "A long time ago," "In a land far away," someone's name, or something as simple as a date. A few sample beginning sentences include:

On July 2, 1997, Bill Jones was . . . .
Many weeks ago, Tom was walking home,
and he was in for the day of his life.

You can also water it down to lower skill levels; for instance, "Many," "Last week," or "There once was (were)." A full beginning sentence might read:

Last week, Bob was having a lot of fun,
but he didn't know it.

After beginnings catch on, we'd start mixing spice with spice. An opening would contain three to four compositional risks.

Many weeks ago, Jack was playing football, and he walked up to his teammates and announced, "Hey guys, are you ready for some football? Let's get ready to rock and roll!"
A few weeks ago, there was a student named Jack Jones; and he said to his class, in an authoritative voice, "Class, I know we can ace this test! Who's with me?"

These beginnings each have a compound sentence, a direct address, a question, figurative language, and a direct quote.

Most of my students used to pick their favorite beginnings and elaborate on them with various kinds of spice. I never held back any gifted writers. If they could do a spicy beginning that I never thought of, then so be it! Now I was learning from them.

7. Endings (potatoes)

I used to tell the kids the ending was the part that would make or break the story. I'd relate to when they were younger and their parents were reading them a bedtime story. I would say:

> *. . . And then Jack walked right-up to that giant and said, '?.' Now, go to sleep and I'll see you tomorrow.*

This kind of ending left them with an empty feeling, and it shows how a weak ending leaves the reader with that same empty feeling. I wanted an ending to add flavor, taste, and SPICE to their story. I always pushed either humor or some kind of "ahhh" ending. For example:

> *Perhaps the Eagles quarterback felt he could've won the game if he had given a better effort on the final play, but he literally found out that birds of a feather do not flock together.*

This kind of ending gives the reader a little chuckle and, ideally, more of a completed feeling. Having endings like this made my job a lot more fun.

Teaching endings usually takes about a week; however, adding more spice will take longer. Simple endings are what I used to call "ending words," e.g. "Finally," "It almost," "Perhaps," "At last," "Maybe," "Although," and "Apparently," just to name a few.

8. Facts and Opinions (oregano)

Facts and opinions progress as the child's grade level and age increase. Facts and opinions are a simple form of spice that can be used in almost any kind of written prompt because everybody has an opinion. I used to just match an opinion to a fact to give the paper a little more flavor, e.g. "It's a fact that _____, but in my opinion I feel. . . ." Many children have trouble with this skill because they believe their opinions are true. This is where you give examples of facts. Teaching facts at first is enhanced by using tangible or concrete objects; something that they can hold on to. Next, an opinion would be an expression of one of their senses: seeing, feeling, tasting, smelling, or hearing.

It is a fact that I'm writing with a pencil, but in my opinion if feels just right.

After a week or so, it slowly catches on. Some facts breed many different opinions. Writing a fact and giving an opinion was actually easier to teach than trying to figure out if a statement was either. For example, is the following sentence a fact or an opinion?

Some people believe walking in the city is a good way to travel.

Believe it or not, it's a fact, because *some* people do. You would find this in a multiple-choice question, and it tends to confuse children, adults, and teachers alike. I really used to dislike these questions because they were not fair to the kids.

9. Homophones and Homographs (parsley)

Homophones and homographs are skills that deal with word variety. I would take them slowly and use many different techniques for each one. For instance, *two, too,* and *to;* the word "too" is confusing at first, so I used to tell the kids they could only use it at the end of a sentence. This would, at least, start them using it correctly. After I felt the students used it consistently, we would go to "too much" and "too many".

The words "they're" and "their" are also often misused by elementary students. I would tell my kids that since "they're" is broken into two pieces, it means two things, places, or people.

The word "their" has an "i" in it, so either "I" own it or someone else does. I found out these tiny little tricks worked because children seem to relate to them. Eventually, we would take a pair of homophones and put them in the same sentence. Dictating sentences is also a good drill because the kids have to spell and punctuate the entire sentence correctly.

Homographs are a little easier to teach because the spellings don't change. Dictating these sentences would help the kids with the double meaning of a word.

The __wind__ was starting to __wind__ down.

This skill was picked up easily.

10. Apostrophes – 's and s' (sage)

This is a skill that used to drive me up a wall – after teaching it, every word that ended in **s** now appeared as **'s**. At first, I would only let them use it if it was on a person's name, e.g. **Bob's** or **Mike's**. After words, we would add describing words, e.g. "**Bob's** blue hat" or "**Tom's** big nose". As for **s'**, for the most part the children had a tough time with this. After trying for years I found out that very few can use this form correctly. I tried to steer clear of this, however; those who could use it were encouraged to do so. Some skills, if used consistently incorrectly, can actually hurt a written piece. If a child wants to use it correctly – and still has problems – tell them to put it on a person's name that ends with the letter **s**, e.g. **Jess'** or **Bess'**, but only use it once to show a spicy risk.

11. Questions (rosemary)

Questions are a simple form of spice, but when used correctly, they can really help a story flow evenly. Many people like to begin a piece with a question, and ideally, it will grab the reader's attention. Using questions with dialogue is another form

25

of spice. It will usually stimulate some kind of response, and can also add a little humor.

> *Bob, frightened, yelled out, "Bill, can you help me?" Bill replied, "Sure, just get off my foot."*
>
> *On July 2, 2007, Johnny U. walked up to his teammates and said, "Team, are we ready? Who's with me?"*

With younger children, you can follow a question with a "yes", "no", or "well" answer to put two thoughts together. This skill develops extra thinking and more complete thoughts while writing.

> *Did mom want me to go to the store? Yes, she did, because I want my favorite kind of cereal.*

I call these "two-fors." You get two longer sentences for one thought, and you can also insert a vocabulary word in one of the sentences.

Rhetorical questions are the next type of questions. These may add flavor with a twist to a piece. They may be introduced as early as fourth grade, but go very slowly for a while. While writing, we have to be authoritative rather than disrespectful.

> *Do you think kids really want to go to school seven days a week?*

Another good example of a rhetorical question can refer to the children's parents. When Mom gets upset and says, "Who do you think you are?" we all know what happens if we answer this kind of question. Using questions is a risk that is not often considered, but when used correctly, it can be very effective.

12. Exclamatory Sentences (thyme)

Using exclamations is another seemingly unnoticed skill that can also enhance children's essays. The exclamation mark, "!", used correctly, is a simple but very effective risk. I would teach it by telling the kids that it is used sparingly. Some children like to put it all over; however, using it only once is better. We would use it on an onomatopoeia word like "BANG!" Or "ZOOM!" Using it more than once may hurt an essay more than help it. I used to tell the kids that they are not yelling their entire story, so use it sparsely.

Using supposal examples helps the children with its usage. I used to use it incorrectly at first to show the power of this risk. For example, if you looked out your window and you saw lightning hit a tree, you wouldn't say, "Wow, lightning." You would say, "WOW, LIGHTNING!" Can you see its power? Just remember that saying it this way is only powerful if it is used once in the entire selection.

13. Transitional Words and Paragraphs (onions)

Transitional words are a great way to teach sequence, paragraphs, and simple three-part essays or stories. This works as far down as second grade, and it is very useful when writing written responses.

Using time-based words such as "first", "next", and "finally" helped my students break a story into three parts. Using these words, along with a beginning and ending, enabled my children to write a five-paragraph story in sequential order. Many persuasive essays, expository stories, and open-ended responses can benefit from this method. Simply add spice to each sentence, and the answer is complete and thorough.

Here is an example of a transitional story using one to explain how to use it. If the story requires more sections, simply add the words "then" and "furthermore" for as many as seven paragraphs.

> *This is how you write a transitional story using transitional words. Add spice when needed and don't forget to indent.*
>
> *First, you write the word "first" followed by a comma, and then explain your initial thought. Always use the word "because" in the sentence to explain your first thought. Make this thought a compound sentence.*
>
> *Next, we use "next" instead of "secondly", because most children — if they use "secondly" — will go right to "third" instead of "finally". Try to make this thought a listing sentence.*
>
> *"Finally" is the last transitional word to use. Don't forget the comma or the word "because". It helps to explain your answer, along with a fact and opinion in this sentence, or another form of spice. Remember that this is not your last sentence in this kind of response.*
>
> *This is your ending paragraph because it is your conclusion, and it organizes, develops, and concludes your essay.*

Please remember that as the grade level increases, so does this skill. What is acceptable in grade three is usually not in the following grade because as each grade increases, so does the level of application.

Remember that if you have a "first", you must also have a "finally" or "lastly" to complete your essay. I used to explain that it was the "English Law". This usually caught on quickly.

If a question asked for as many as five reasons, things, ideas, or thoughts, it was handled using *first, next, then, again* or *furthermore,* and *finally* or *lastly.*

Other kinds of transitional words and phrases could be the spatial type, e.g. "in the background", "a sound from above", or "lurking from underneath." These can also signal a new paragraph.

Transitional words can be used in many styles to enhance writing skills. Settling a conflict and resolving it using *first, next,* and *finally* is an extremely effective way to show risk.

First, the man thought about it. Next, he knew what he had to do. Finally, he did it, and it worked as good as gold.

Making paragraphs is a skill that should be monitored closely because many children make these transitions. This skill needs to be drilled while conferencing with the child and – depending on the grade level – taught accordingly. Most children up to grades five or six make new paragraphs when they think it's time to put one. Is it? Usually not; however, after seven or eight lines, they just put one. Their philosophy is: "It looks like a new place for a paragraph, so I'd better put one." This is very confusing to children, and explaining this is even harder.

Using dialogue is a sneaky way to start a new paragraph. In second, third, and fourth grade I always taught that direct quotes initiated a new paragraph. Simply put, "DQ (NP)". Each grade level was the barometer for how many paragraphs: Second grade needed two, third grade needed three, and so on.

Many people and textbooks tend to teach a topic sentence, and then use this to initiate a paragraph. I found teaching paragraphs backwards works better. Putting two sentences that go together was a way to get started. Instead of putting one spelling word in each sentence, I would require two sentences that go together using a spelling word only once. This is the beginning of a paragraph. For example, if the spelling word is "unhelpful", a student may write:

> *Bill was trying to help his mother, but it was not easy. He realized he was <u>unhelpful</u> at first because he was all thumbs. After he got himself on track, it was a piece of cake.*

After the beginning sentences, we go to three sentences that are aligned with each other, and so on. Now I have a bunch of supporting details with only one spelling word, but they all are on one topic. Now we work on a topic sentence. This works from the inside of a paragraph and helps the student put a paragraph together.

Try not to get too involved with this skill. Also, make sure they indent using two fingers only. Some kids like to indent half way down the line, or some kids put one word on the initial line. They just want to show you that they are indenting. I used to call this overkill, and catching it quickly helps eliminate this problem.

14. Dialogue and Direct Quotes (hot sauce)

Dialogue is a skill that, if introduced too early, can really bring a written assignment into disarray. This skill may be introduced as early as first grade – sometimes even kindergarten. Some children get it, but many do not. Before teaching, or re-teaching it, you should set limits on how much dialogue you expect. I used to explain that until this skill is taught, nobody should talk in their stories. Tell the story as a narrator, and that's it. Sometimes I had to teach how *not* to use dialogue before I actually began teaching this skill. At first, I taught the kids that using the word "that" will actually let someone talk without direct quotes; for instance, "Bob said that he wants to go to the store."

No quotation marks are needed here. When this skill is internalized, the child is ready to go.

I never held back gifted children that could use this skill effectively; however, up to grade six, many children still had trouble using it. Misuse has to be addressed early when you conference with the child. Generally, it slowly improves as the year progresses.

The purpose of limiting its use is because many children like to make conversation, and at times, it gets too confusing to read or to grade. For example:

> *Bob said I want to go over here. No you don't. Yes I do. Well then come here first.*

This entire section was written with no direct quotes, and now I have to grade it: Now what? I used to circle the whole section and put a big "DQ?". This child had to plan when to use dialogue and how to use it sparingly.

Another time-saving technique with direct quote usage is always to put the speaker at the beginning of the sentence.

> *Bob said, "Come here."*

Putting the speaker's name at the end of a sentence requires five to six more skills. After the children master this, then we go to putting the name last, or even in the middle of a sentence.

> *"I like to eat ice cream," said Jack.*
> *"I like," said Jack, "to eat some ice cream."*

Notice how confusing this is to teach. Putting the correct punctuation for dialogue and using it in various ways should depend on the level of the child's ability. You can determine this during individual conferencing. I also have a unique way of teaching direct quotes. I called them "little sixes" and "little nines". If you look at them, that is exactly what they look like. For every set of sixes, there is a set of nines. I taught them to actually say the word "sixes" for the initial quotation marks and "nines" for the final ones.

Jack said, "I want some cake."
Jack said (comma) (sixes) I want some cake (period) (nines).

Most of the time, they would remember the sixes but forget the nines. Saying them was actually a way to help proofread their own work. As the year progresses, so does this skill. I would let my enriched children put two sentences inside a dialogue sentence.

Bill said, "I like it here! This is a real nice place."

To add more spice to the dialogue, simply replace the word "said" with a different word, such as *yelled, screamed, replied, cried out,* or another phrase.

Bob yelled out, "COME HERE!"

Notice the spice and the flavor of this sentence. Why is it capitalized? He is *yelling* it. The child should only write this kind of exclamatory sentence once or twice in a story.

Bob replied, in an extremely angry voice, "I want you here, right now!"

This kind of dialogue helps create the mood in your story, and it helps to build character traits. I specifically named this skill hot sauce because too much of it will hurt the flavor of the written assignment.

15. Addressing Sentences (adobo)

Addressing sentences sometimes give the students trouble because of their nature. This problem can be corrected immediately by changing them into questions.

Bob, can you come here?

Many times, children will put a person's name at the beginning and get confused, thinking that this must be an addressing sentence, because that's their new skill this week. As you can see, this is often used incorrectly.

Bill, walked to the store.

Also, putting the name first helps because it stands out in a question.

Bill, can I walk to the store too?
Class, would you please stand?

This skill lends itself to being placed in a dialogue sentence, and if introduced this way, I call it putting spice inside of spice.

Bill asked, "Bob, can you come here, or are you going to stay there?"

Notice not only is this an addressing sentence, but it is a compound question inside a direct quote. This is triple spice, and it is very effective.

16. Yes, No, Well (sugar)

Another skill that uses a comma is a sentence beginning with "yes", "no", or "well". This is a skill that usually appears in the comma section of language books. If not separated and taught as a different skill, it is often used incorrectly.

Separating each skill and requiring a comma needs to be taught by itself in order for the child to feel more confident while writing and to spice up a story or composition. The words "yes", "no", and "well" can be put in direct quotes or simply used by themselves.

> *Yes, he knew he had, but he didn't want to tell anybody.*
> *Ben screamed out, "Yes, we won!"*
> *The little boy was looking for his mom, but he couldn't find her. Well, now he had to walk home, and he was upset, hungry, and very tired.*

Please note that as the skill level increases, so does the complexity of the sentence structure created by adding spice to spice. In the third example above, the final sentence is a complex sentence and can be used in the upper grades.

Well, I hope using this skill helps your students, and yes, I am using it right now to show you how to use it. This is what spice does to the reader. It gives them a little jolt or giggle while reading a selection.

17. Spice –in– Spice (all spice)

As you can probably already tell, I have been putting various kinds of sentences into others. I call this skill "spice-in-spice." This is when you get your students to really start writing with ease. The flow of the written process becomes smooth, fun to read, and extremely well-written. Now you can take off with your students and start to soar. By this time, most of your students are writing well, but you will always have a few that will struggle.

Let these children do what they can. Some skills may be out of their reach, so you should let them attempt them slowly. Let them attempt skills they are comfortable with in order to build confidence. I know it's hard sometimes, but remember that all kids need a fair chance to succeed. Teachers make a big difference in a child's perception of whether or not he or she can, or cannot, do something well.

Individual student/teacher conferencing can actually help a child's writing skill grow from one paper to the next. Watch the child's face when you give individual compliments about their writing. They just light up! You will discover how to give confidence and proficiency and also create a special bond between you and your students while conferencing.

Spice-in-spice has to be closely monitored at first because some students get too carried away. For some, it becomes a contest of how much spice they can put into a sentence. Just remember, too much of one kind of spice is not a good thing.

As time moves on, you get sentences that are grade levels ahead of the student, and you become amazed at their growth. Here are some examples of spice-in-spice:

> *Tom was so excited after winning that he seemed to be happy as a lark, flying high on cloud nine, and just sitting on top of the world.*
>
> *Jack screamed out, "Bill, are you for real, or do you have no common sense?"*
>
> *On July 2, 2007, Johnny Football was getting ready to play in the Super Bowl, and he fearlessly walked up to his teammates and blurted out, "Team, are we ready to go kick some butt? Let's rock-n-roll!"*
>
> *The players were so excited, revved-up, and psyched that they all rushed to the door and literally tore it off of its hinges.*

Certain spice should only be used once in a story.

> *Tom rattled out, "HELP!" (Does this look like Tom is rattled?)*
>
> *Tom screamed out, "HELP ME!" (Is he yelling this? Is this a compositional risk? I think so, but remember to do this only once in a written selection.)*
>
> *"Charlie, get over here now," cried Tom, "because I need to tell you about this situation!"*

Advanced levels of spice-in-spice can be used if applicable, as shown in the sentence above. Gifted writers can use this for advanced proficiency, and a sentence like the third example above is extremely effective.

No matter how well a child picks up the spice skill of dialogue, remember that it is called "hot sauce" because too much of it hurts a story. If not used correctly, the reader can get lost in some transitions. Monitor dialogue closely and try not to teach it until the students can actually "tell" a story. Most papers need to be narrated, not spoken. It's not how many dialogue sentences are used, but where you put them that makes a difference.

18. Titles (basil)

Not all written pieces require a title, but I feel most do, especially when writing a narrative, speculative, or an expository. After all, teachers are supposed to teach children lifetime skills, and hopefully those skills will remain in place from year-to-year. If all teachers require titles, the stories will not change much from one grade to the next. While I was teaching, I was informed that some written tests do not need a title. I did not want to teach to a test. I wanted to teach my children how to write, and just about every fictional piece that I have seen had had a title. I not only required a title, but we added a little spice to it. Titles were done in alliterations. Using this kind of titles eliminated the question of which words in a title need to be capitalized. Many children in younger grades have trouble with capitalization in titles.

The Big and Fun Trip to the City

This is a long title, but I think you can see my point. Start with two words at first: <u>Gary's Game</u>, <u>Bouncing Billy</u>, <u>Mike's Machine</u>.

Then move on to three word examples: <u>Bobby's Big Bash</u>, <u>Murphy's Mighty Moment</u>, <u>Jay's Jumping Jacks</u>.

The child should either underline or put quotes around the title. I suggest you stay consistent. I made my students underline alliterated titles because it makes them stand out and adds a twist to their stories.

19. Sequence (paprika)

Everything that occurs during the day happens in sequence. We all know it, but trying to get children to retell a situation, or a story, is sometimes difficult. There are gaps in their stories, and events get left out. Sometimes these events are necessary to understand what has happened. For example, after an argument happens, you have two students explaining what went on, and you get two different stories. After everything comes out, it finally makes sense.

When teaching sequence, children need to use a web or graphic organizer. Putting things in order by writing them down relieves the mind of confusing sequential thoughts.

Title: <u>Gary's Game</u>
1. The team was getting ready.
2. Fans were excited.
3. The game started.
4. We played hard.

5. *We almost won.*
6. *We lost.*
7. *We were sad.*
8. *We got over it.*

This is the sequential planning needed while writing a situational, narrative, or speculative story.

Make sure picture prompts are about the picture and stay on the same topic throughout the story. This enables the child to stay on target. The children should use every part of the picture if possible.

For younger children, the preparation of food is an excellent way to teach sequence. This is where transitional stories come in to play using time-based words, such as *first, next, then, again, furthermore,* and *finally.*

The process of making a peanut butter and jelly sandwich works very well. I would purposely make it backwards or incorrect, and my students would tell me what I was doing out of order. Putting it in order using transition words makes more sense.

> *This is how to make a peanut butter and jelly sandwich. First, take two slices of bread and place them on a plate. Next, spread peanut butter on one slice and jelly on the other. Then, you put them together. Finally, you have your sandwich. That is how to make a peanut butter and jelly sandwich.*

This example is for elementary school, but it can be adapted for middle school using more challenging food preparation skills.

20. Conflict and Resolution (celery salt)

How many stories, movies, real life situations, or novels have some kind of conflict/resolution scenario? Just about every situation has some kind of problem, and how it is handled or solved is usually the climax or conclusion. At times, there are even small conflicts within other conflicts that need to be dealt with immediately before moving on.

> *You need something in the basement, but you can't see because there is no light down there. The light gets replaced, but now you blew a fuse. You have no fuses and . . . .*

I'm sure you get the idea. It's like the domino effect, and there are many conflicts that need to be resolved before the original conflict can be resolved.

Do all conflicts in stories need to have happy endings? No, but they need to end one way or another. Stay away from "to be continued" because it leaves the reader with an empty feeling.

While resolving something, slide a set of transitional words into the answer to help the writer. This gives a three-part mini-story within the prompt or essay. It is very effective, and teaching this will definitely increase the length of a written piece.

> *This is what I did. First, I went to . . . Next, it worked so well . . . Finally, this was even better than . . . .*

Now you are really spicing things up. You can also put other kinds of spice inside these transitional sentences. This is spice-in-spice once again.

Since this skill is also a character education standard, maybe we can do a little cross-teaching and have our students explain how they have handled their past conflicts. It definitely won't hurt explaining how to deal with new situations that arise during the year.

21. Similarities and Differences (cumin)

Similarities and differences are skills used in many open-ended questions, books, and tests. This skill is taught from kindergarten to college and used in many other subjects and disciplines. It only has to be used once because it sets the stage for character traits, the mood in a story, and attitude and behavior. Some children enjoy this skill because they can use themselves, or anyone they choose. Only use one or two sentences when introducing this skill.

He was funny like me, but he was different because he was a lot older.

Bob was like no other person I had ever seen. He was always happy go-lucky, extremely enthusiastic, and always keeping me on my toes with his witty comments.

This skill is also used in Science, Social Studies, Math, Music, and Art classes, but it takes on different various meanings with its use. This skill was destined, in my opinion, to be cross-taught in many ways. In Science, we would discuss it with the properties and characteristics; Social Studies, the different regions throughout the state, country, and world; Math, to compare angles, shapes, and estimated answers; and any other way that worked. It was a great way to manage time while teaching.

Writing with spice should be required throughout the disciplines so that everyone in the school will be on the same page and will all have similar expectations. The "writing risks" or "spice" stays the same, but we just gear it to the subject.

22. Humor (lemon balm)

Humor usually gives the teacher, or reader, a little chuckle while reading an essay or prompt. This skill can be inserted by using rhetorical questions, figurative language, or dialogue.

> *Weren't you a kid in school once?*
> *Aren't we supposed to listen to experts?*
> *The little boy was uptight, out of sight, but in the groove during the game.*
> *Today, I got up on the wrong side of the bed, and I felt like ten miles of bad road.*
> *Billy literally jumped out of his shoes and replied, "You almost scared me out of my skin, too!"*

Humor is used in many ways, and as long as the child doesn't over-do it, it has its place in most prompts. It's a definite compositional risk because it usually comes out in several different spices. How will you know if a sentence has humor in it? If you laugh or smirk while reading a child's story, so will other readers of your students' work.

23. Spice for the Enriched Child (pick your own spice)

Colons, semicolons, and hyphenated words are skills for middle and high school students. These forms of spice can be infused into writing as the teacher sees fit. These skills are used only to spice up an essay or story, not to dominate it. It is usually up to the teacher to determine how much of a specific skill can be used at first so the child doesn't get too carried away. Other forms of advanced spice include personification, flashback, and foreshadowing. Each one of these skills can be used with other forms of spice to enhance the level of writing. Notice how the first example below contains flashback, figurative language, and a compound sentence.

Tom knew he would have trouble with it because he had tried it before, but he wanted to give it a shot anyway. (flashback)

As we walked through the city, the tall buildings glared like still giants, but we figured out how to walk quietly beneath them. (personification)

Children, from time to time, put many things in their stories, but the teacher has to control where stories lead. Please try *not* to encourage any kind of violent behavior in their writing. Many kids write about people getting hurt or passing away. I try to discourage this type of writing because I feel it is not appropriate for children. At times, the children will experiment with certain forms of life-or-death situations. My response was, "Nobody dies or gets injured in your stories."

Johnny was so scared that he kicked the bucket.

I'd explain that instead of kicking the bucket, let's say that he *almost* kicked the bucket, or he wasn't even close to kicking the bucket. This is a better way of using this figurative language expression.

In today's world, violence is not acceptable, and writing violent things has to be put on the back shelf. Besides, you never know who is going to read your students' papers.

II. Drilling and Internalizing Spice

24. Dictation

Dictation is an activity that helps the student to comprehend the purpose of punctuation. I'd simply dictate spicy sentences, and the child had to put correct capitalization and punctuation for the entire sentence. For example:

bill walks to the store and he buys some soda candy and cupcakes

After dictating this sentence, I would write it on the board with no capitals or punctuation. Then we would slowly go through each possible mistake and check it. Each child would circle the possible mistake and put a "c" if correctly given or an "x" if not.

c or x bill walks to the store c or x, and he buys some soda c or x, candy c or x, and cupcakes c or x.

This sentence has about five possible mistakes. We would do about two or three of these exercises each day, depending on which spice skill we were working with that week. If I put a spelling word in the dictated sentence, it had to be written correctly. As the year progresses, you can put as much spice as you wish in a dictated sentence. For example:

on july 2 2008 jack jones was reading my paper and he blurted out this is the best paper I have ever seen in my life

There are about twelve possible mistakes in this beginning sentence.

Sometimes switching papers helps with this kind of drilling because children are tough graders. Some kids would say, "Mr. D, she forgot to dot her I. Is this wrong?" My response was, "Do I count it when you don't?"

Always put the number of incorrect responses at the end of a dictated sentence. It helps home in on mistakes. For example:

> *bob eats breakfast lunch and dinner every day*
> *Bob eats breakfast, lunch, and dinner every day. - 0 (This is out of four possible correct answers — if they missed one then I'd write -1, and so on.)*

After about four days, I would collect their papers and use it for a quiz. Each quiz would contain between sixty and one hundred possible errors.

25. Cut and Paste

Children sometimes have trouble thinking of what to write about in sentences. They'd say, "I can't think of anything!" That is where this activity kicks in.

Cut out a picture from a magazine, paste it on a lined piece of paper, and have them write a spiced-up sentence about the picture. This activity automatically increases sentence length and gives them a purpose for writing. If I inserted one of their spelling words, then the sentence would be used as both a language and a spelling grade.

You can use as many various spiced-up sentences as you wish for a picture. Any picture works for any spice given. You can have as many as five separate spicy sentences for one picture.

Example:
Spelling word: <u>carefully</u>

1.   *Bill and his family work <u>carefully</u> on their farm, and they always have a fruitful crop.*
2. It was a fact that Bill was a farmer, but in his opinion, he was the most <u>carefully</u> trained farmer in the state of New Jersey.
3.   A few weeks ago, Bill Jones <u>carefully</u> plowed his fields, and he explained, "This is how you do it correctly."

Grading these papers was more fun than just reading sentences because the children would sometimes write very creative sentences about the picture. You could also have the child simply draw a picture and write about it, because many students love to draw. I call this activity "Draw and Write".

26. Word for the Day

This is a drilling activity that is a real eye-opener for your students. After writing sentences about pictures, the following activity falls right into place. "Word for the Day" shows your students how far they have come because it uses many forms of spice already covered. I would have my students cut out any picture they wish and begin to write short stores without them knowing it.

I'd explain that first, I would want some kind of beginning sentence about the picture. Next, they would try to write a sentence about similar details in the picture, and then make this into a compound sentence. Then the third sentence would stay together with the first two, but now I would want a listing sentence. Finally, they would add an ending sentence, and voila: They have written their first speculative picture narrative, and they don't even know it.

Adding a variety of vocabulary words was the next step. This activity could be used for any kind of prompt. Simply adjust it to the level of the student.

Example: Word – <u>Area</u>

Last year, Jack Jones was playing a game with his team. His football field had a big area, and he used every inch of it. The field was wide, long, and very hard. Jack tried his best, but his team lost. Perhaps he will win next time.

This story has a beginning, varied sentences, a variety of words, and an ending. Notice the flow of the story and the transitions, along with a beginning and an ending. Other kinds of prompts also work the same way.

27. Drilling for Speculative and Persuasive Essays

Drilling for speculative and persuasive essays is almost done the same way, but instead of using pictures, use situations, for instance: Write five compound, listing, or fact/opinion sentences about why students should have homework every night including the weekend – or write five why they shouldn't. Notice the topics. I try to give my students topics that they like or dislike. Always hit a topic from all sides so that their writing becomes universal. Situation drills can be used with any kind of spice and on any range of topics.

> *Tom lost his wallet. What now?*
> *Persuade your teacher to let you have Friday off.*

Speculative writing come in many varieties; however, most are exactly what they say. The students speculate or guess what they think is going on and write about it. Instead of having to look at a picture, they are given the situation. The main idea is also given, but many times it is general or vague. This is because the child has to fill in the rest and elaborate. More elaboration makes for a better story.

The story can be either actual or fiction. I suggest going with fiction because the child can use their imagination and make up as many details as they wish. In order to tell a complete story and have all the bases covered, I wanted the children to include three basic parts: characters, situation, and how to handle or deal with the situation. Here is a simple example:

> *While walking home, a child found a wallet lying on the ground. It was full of money and credit cards. What did the child do? Write a story about the child, his situation, and how he handles or deals with it.*

Explain to your students that you want three separate parts in their stories. The first part is the character; second, the situation; and finally, how the situation is dealt with accordingly.

A few weeks ago, Jack was walking home from baseball practice, and he was in for the time of his life. Jack was a really good child, very honest, and always as happy as a kid on his birthday. It was a fact that he was in fifth grade, but in his opinion he was an extremely responsible student.

A little while later, Jack had his head down while walking, and he couldn't believe his eyes! There, in front of him, was a wallet full of money and several credit cards. Jack rhetorically thought, "What should I do? Is being honest a good thing?"

All of a sudden, BING! A light bulb went off in his head, and Jack knew exactly what to do. First, he looked around to see if he saw anyone looking for something. Next, just by chance, he noticed a patrol car slowly coming down the street. Finally, he waved down the police and told them what happened, and they took it from there. Maybe the person who lost the wallet was upset, but Jack made sure he did the right thing. Perhaps the wallet's owner will give Jack a reward, but Jack's pride was boosted that day because he believes that what goes around comes around.

This is a short three-part situation narrative, or speculative. Notice the spice: a beginning, compound sentences, listing sentences, figurative language, apostrophes, affixes, fact/opinion, transitional words, onomatopoeia, and an ending, just to name a few.

Every time a student uses one of these words, they should use a synonym the next time. A persuasive essay must also use believable circumstances and statistics. Usually between forty and sixty percent is a believable percentage, considering your point of view and the topic given. Listing parts from most important to least seems to work best; however, it's up to the teacher. A persuasive essay's range of use is unlimited, and its power can demonstrate a lifelong writing skill to your students.

Persuasive essays – or letters – are used to display an authoritative, commanding and convincing writing style. The writer needs to take a stand and not be indecisive or derogatory with their points of view. They need to take their strategy personally, along with two more convincing aspects. These ideas can take many forms and can be fabricated, but they also need to be **believable**. High powered examples like: doctors, experts, scientists, congressmen, governors, mayors, city councilmen. And studies and statistics: monetary, ethical, moral, physical, athletics and any other powerful purposes and people. This essay should be five paragraphs long with about five spicy sentences in each paragraph.

Here is an example of a topic:
The President has decided to make Saturday school mandatory. What is your reaction to this decision? Write a letter to explain your point of view on the decision.

Initially attack the assignment and underline key words like the words **letter** and **President** in order to stay focused. Sometimes the test says write an "essay," so do not be fooled.

Now we plan our writing assignment by making two columns and planning our thoughts.

Example:

My three perspectives are: personally, expert, and studies from famous Children's Hospital laboratories.

Always try to go from most important to least.

Topic: School All Year Long

positive	negative
1. Smarter	1. No time off
2. ?	2. Depressing attitude
3.	3. No fun time
4.	4. No friend time
	5. No money
	Dr. Jones
	Stats

Just add your spice acronym and begin your five paragraphs. **Please note beginnings and endings bend to the essay, do not use any empty expressions.**

Sample beginnings: I understand, It has come to my attention, or I have recently been informed.

Sample endings: In conclusion, All in all, To sum it up, or In summation.

Here is a skeleton of a persuasive essay.

Dear Sir,

I understand that you _____;
however, doing this would _____. First, I
have personal _____. Next, experts also
_____. Finally, studies and statistics
from _____ reveal that _____. Please

consider these aspects before you set your plan in cement.

> *To begin with I have personal_____.*
> *Saturday is my day to play football, baseball, and basketball because _____. I also have a job to _____. Don't you think I should help my family pay the bills?*
>
> *Secondly, Dr. Jones with degrees from Harvard University and Princeton University has recently stated, "_____" and "_____." (Make him say two things.) Aren't we supposed to listen to doctors? Many other experts also _____, and _____. It's a fact that _____, and in their opinions_____.*
>
> *Lastly, studies from Children's Hospital show that 44% of children who attended Saturday school end up living at home longer than the students who attended school five days a week. Do you think _____? They also reveal _____.*
>
> *In conclusion I would like to reiterate the several _____. Saturday school _____, _____, _____, and _____. Perhaps going to school six days a week _____, but you were a kid once, have a heart!*
>
> *Respectfully,*
>
> _____*(your name)*

Notice the word variety. Always mix it up and try to never repeat words twice. This is where a synonym spelling section comes into play. Notice the six transitional words or phrases used in this letter. This letter is authoritative, not nasty. Just make sure your words are powerful with no empty expressions, like: *It seems to me,* <u>or</u> *for the reason that.* These expressions are **not** powerful.

This kind of writing style will be a lifelong skill for your children and prepare them for any written test down the road, because persuasive writing is one of the most tested areas of writing in America.

III. Planning for Stories, Prompts, and Essays

28. Graphic Organizers and Webs

Different essays or stories require various types of planning. The trick is to keep it simple, and that is the direction you want to take. A picture prompt needs story elements in order to come up with a main idea. Here is an example:

Story elements: Who, what, when, why, where, how, because. (For K, 1 & 2, keep the story elements to who and what. This starts the child thinking and usually stimulates parts of when, where, and why.)

Main idea:

Title: (Alliteration)

(Planning is done in sequence using the picture.)

1. Beginning	5. Direct quote
2. Compound sentences	6. Affixes
3. Listing	7. 's
4. Fact/opinion	8. Ending

Now add spice and start writing your story. Use the same basic method for a speculative; however, remember that the theme of the article is already given. This is a three-paragraph planning web for a narrative speculative:

Paragraph 1: Character(s)

1. _____ Beginning, compound, idiom
2. _____ Listing
3. _____ Fact/opinion
4. _____ 's
5. _____ Prefix (dialogue)

Paragraph 2: The situation

6. _____ A little later (new paragraph)
7. _____ Rhetorical question
8. _____ ! Exclamation
9. _____ Listing
10._____ Dialogue (new paragraph)

Paragraph 3: The handling or dealing with the situation

11._____ Onomatopoeia! (new paragraph)
12._____ Transitional words (first, next, lastly)
13._____ Compound sentence
14._____ Pre-ending maybe (affixes)
15._____ Ending, compound sentence, figure of speech

Putting dialogue at the end of the first and second planned section generates two more paragraphs and shows even more spice. I found that as a child uses each section of the web, crossing out used parts keeps them on task. Also, crossing out completed sections shows progress and gives the child a feeling of accomplishment.

Persuasive essays use a different planning technique because you need to list your points of view.

I like it because: I dislike it because:

1.   1.
2.   2.
3.   3.
                            4. Dr. Jones (expert's point of view)
                            5. Statistics (student research)

Whichever column has more reasons is the better choice. Just add spice and begin writing your five-paragraph essay.

29. Spice Acronym

Adding spice to any situation is the key to displaying a student's writing ability. The spice acronym does just that, and it is written on the planning page. This is how it goes: "I begin and end all long compositions for fantastic teachers down here right away." This is memorized and listed downward on the planning page. As the child uses each kind of spice, they simply check it off to prevent overuse of any one skill.

Once a child uses spice twice, they must move to another skill. Different spices can be used as often as three times. This keeps sentence structure changing throughout the written selection. Writing the acronym vertically helps students to understand it:

I	SPICE	Indent #? (1 - 5 times)
Begin	(meat)	Beginning sentence
And	(chives)	Affixes, prefixes, suffixes
End	(potatoes)	Ending sentence
All	(sage)	Apostrophes
Long	(oregano)	Listing sentence
Compositions	(salt)	Compound: words, subjects/predicates, sentences
For	(pepper)	Figurative language
Fantastic	(garlic)	Fact/opinion
Teachers	(onions)	Transitional words: First, next, lastly
Down	(hot sauce)	Dialogue (new paragraph)
Here	(parsley)	Homophones, homographs
Right	(rosemary)	Rhetorical questions
Away		Anything else, depending on the level of the writer: Flashback, foreshadowing, personification, conflict/resolution, humor, colons, semi-colons, hyphenated sentences, similarity and differences, compare and contrast, and so on. . .

For younger children, I would use vegetables instead of spices because some children don't understand what different spices do to foods. Use salt, pepper, meat, potatoes, tomatoes, carrots, onions, celery, and peppers. It's less confusing and keeps things simple.

Older children love to experiment and spice up their food on occasion. They can convert it into writing by sprinkling many spices all over their foods.

Elementary teachers should use whichever parts of the acronym they can. Here is a basic pace chart for each grade level:

Kindergarten/ First:
I   **Indent**
B   **Beginning sentence**
A   **Anything you can get, or affixes**
E   **Ending sentences**

Second grade continues:
A   **Apostrophes**
L   **Listing sentences**
C   **Compound subjects, predicates, words, sentences**
F   **Figurative language**

Third grade and up to high school:
F   **Fact/opinion**
T   **Transitional words**
D   **Dialogue (new paragraph)**
H   **Homophones, homographs**
R   **Rhetorical or regular questions**
A   **Any advanced skill taught**

For kindergarten, the first four letters are usually not attempted until mid-year. The concept of a beginning, middle, and ending needs to be nurtured from the start. As an example, indent first, write a beginning sentence, ask a question, answer it with an exclamation, and finally end your story.

Last week, Bob's mom went to the store. Did he want to go, too? Yes, because Bob wanted cereal. Finally, he went to the store and was as happy as a clown.

Notice how this simple story has a beginning, middle, and ending – along with appropriate grade level spice. Just plug in the ability of your class and go from there. As the child plans, he adds "a little bit of this and a little bit of that . . . a little bit of this and a little bit of that."

NOW the reader can eat the paper with his eyes!

This gives the child the idea to add only a little bit of each spice until their paper starts to take on a spicy flavor.

IV. Conferencing and Grading Papers

30. Jack Jones

Jack Jones is the mythical, magical person who has the infamous task of reading and grading our papers once we ship our tests away. His job is to be as subjectively objective as possible and to grade our papers with a rubric. I've given him a name because it gives him a face, and when he has a face, it's more meaningful to everyone. I can always say things like: "Wow, Jack would love this!" or, "Do you think Jack would get lost in this part?"

Using Jack was a way to help my kids focus through many assignments because they took him personally. This is when they spiced up their writing to the next level. From time to time, I would explain to my students that I was going to grade their papers like Jack today. This was test time, and now they wrote like champions and were ready for anything.

Most teachers can identify a student's writing ability before they finish reading their paper. This is the purpose of starting strong, staying spicy, and ending that way. You have to grab hold of Jack and literally make him feel astonished with your first four or five sentences. Jack needs to be admired because he probably reads hundreds of papers in a day. I needed a break after reading five, and depending on the papers, that was sometimes a struggle. Do not feel bad if you bury a few children's papers in the pile at times because you need to read a fairly good one at first. This sets a helpful standard, and sharing this paper with the class will inspire many.

31. Conferencing

Sitting down next to the student and reviewing his or her written papers is a powerful feedback technique. How many times has someone actually done this with you? If you attempt this with your students, you will see steady growth from one written assignment to the next. Many teachers individually grade an essay by putting comments next to various mistakes, circling misused words, and correcting spelling errors. Usually the child looks at the grade given and barely scans the mistakes noted. Did they learn anything? Yes: that they need to try harder next time.

32. Keepers and Fixers

Keepers and Fixers is a conferencing technique designed to home in on both the positive and the negative parts of any written assignment. The teacher and the student simply sit down together and go through the child's paper one sentence at a time. It usually takes, on average, about five minutes, but it is worth its weight in gold. As you and the student go through the work, you are able to understand how and why a child writes in a particular style. You can actually demonstrate how to write thoughts on paper and use different kinds of spice. This is where you and the student become part of the paper and create a special bond, and together you point their writing in the correct direction.

Misused or incorrect spelling often becomes self-evident because most children consistently misspell the same words from one story to the next. You can also encourage positive, well-written sections and improve on any spice skill attempted. Giving praise and building confidence is a <u>must</u> because instead of just homing in on the mistakes and the opportunities for improvement, it takes into account all the positive aspects of an essay. Having the child keep the well-written parts of a paper is just as important as allowing them to fix their mistakes. They start to realize that even though the paper needs work, there are many parts that they did well. Explaining the positive parts of a written piece will help the student realize that their teacher thinks they can write well. Now the students start to believe in themselves, and that is what teachers want.

Sometimes, finding spare time to conference is difficult; however, the benefits are extremely productive and long-lasting. Telling a child how proud you are of various sections of a written piece is an eye-opening and self-motivating factor that continues all year long. Grading by conferencing one-on-one is almost like having an individual education plan (IEP) for every child in your classroom. Sharing certain parts of every child's paper with the class also builds confidence.

Simply write the word "share" next to certain sections and watch the child light up. Always try to do this with everyone in your class from time to time, because every child does something well. As teachers, we seem to dwell on mistakes, but giving positive comments brings out the best in our kids.

Here is an example of Keepers and Fixers. All comments get written in the margin and pointed out in the selection.

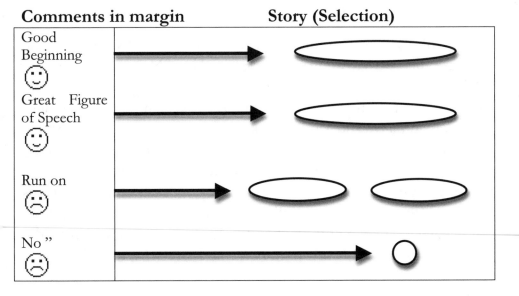

Comments in margin	Story (Selection)
Good Beginning ☺	
Great Figure of Speech ☺	
Run on ☹	
No " ☹	

As we co-read the paper, each student sees the positive and negative parts of their written piece, and so does the teacher. Explaining misspelled words, missing parts, and poorly written sentences allows the child to begin self-correcting immediately. Positives are also evident, and learning takes on a different direction. After conferencing, the child takes a separate piece of paper, folds it in half (long way), and writes "Keepers" on one side and "Fixers" on the other.

Example:

Keepers	Fixers
1. Good beginning	1. Watch run on
2. Good fig. of speech	2. No nines
3. Good Listing	3.
4. Good 's	
5. Great fact/opinion	

All positive comments are written on the **"Keepers"** side because this is what we want the kids to keep. Negatives go on the **"Fixers"** side. Please do not write too many Fixers at first because it becomes overwhelming. Take the most evident mistakes initially, and slowly tackle the rest as you see fit. Staple this paper to their story and give it back before they start the next story. Have them start to keep their Keepers and fix their Fixers. Write the Fixers as in-depth as necessary, as each child's mistakes will be different. Now you will see improvement because the child knows what to keep and what to fix. From one assignment to the next, you will see an improvement, and the writers will start to self-correct their work. Keepers start getting longer, and Fixers become shorter.

For the initial four writing assignments, I usually grade the child against himself, and if improvement is evident, then their grade also increases. This is another self-motivating technique that works on all levels.

Usually after four completed papers, grading their work as a whole class comes into play. This is when I start grading like Jack Jones and most of the class is writing proficiently.

By January, many children are writing at levels above their abilities and are ready to tackle any writing assignment with ease. Grading papers now becomes fun, and their work is better and spicier than ever. Around test time, many children are proficient and feel that writing is now no longer a dreaded task. Many students write so well that you may have to "teach down" to a test because of space limitations on standardized tests. I have had to ask students to check the number of given pages allotted for writing before taking a test and to make sure they know where the final page ends. This way they know where to start their ending paragraph so they will have enough room for a complete, spicy ending.

Keepers and Fixers can also be used for Math problem solving, Science open-ended questions, and any other writing assignment.

Many of the strategies mentioned in this book were designed to actually allow the teacher and student to control a rubric rather than letting it control your teaching methods. After using the strategies in this book, make sure you bend them to your own teaching style and make them work for you.

Each and every class you educate has its own personality, but no matter what, **you** are the teacher, and **you** make a difference.

V. Other Prompts

33. Poem-Linked Prompts

Writing a response for a poem prompt usually draws on a child's past experiences but requires some imagination. It is similar to an expository with extra details added in. The poem that precedes the writing activity is usually linked to the assignment but is different for many children to comprehend. Many times the poem needs to be placed aside following the reading, and explaining the actual writing assignment becomes necessary. This is because many times the poem is a published poem by a well-known author and is far beyond the child's reading ability. Many teachers also have some difficulty understanding the hidden meaning of the poem and require them to take it with a grain of salt and move on.

The poem prompt is almost like a glorified open-ended question with no anthology, and the answers need to come from the student. The section or questions that need to be answered are usually in an expository-type paragraph followed by various bulleted questions. Some bullets have hidden questions within them, so careful reading is a must. Look for words that end in "s" and phrases that include the word "and", as this usually means that more than one answer is required to complete the question. Place the number of questions next to each bullet so that the child knows how many answers are required. Practice this skill as often as possible.

The beginning and ending sentences are taken from the initial paragraph following the poem and should be spiced up in order to grab hold of the reader. Depending on the student, each bullet can be used as a separate paragraph. Here is an example of a poem prompt:

Puddles by Mike Devono

A few days ago I was walking home.
While walking I saw a puddle,
But it was frozen solid.
As I stepped on it, I found it to
Be hard and cold.
A little later I came back.
This time the puddle wasn't frozen
Anymore, so I walked in it again.
This time as my foot left the puddle,
It took with it some of it.
As I get to know people, I hope
To meet them like a puddle.
Not frozen but wet.
So when I leave them I can take
A little of them with me.

Assignment:
As the poem's author meets people, he wants to get to know them. Has there ever been a time when you wanted to meet someone or make friends? Was it hard to talk to them at first? Name someone you wanted to meet once and explain how it happened.
(# of questions — there are six questions within these bullets that need to be answered)
1-• Who was the person?
2-• Was it hard to talk to them, and were they willing to talk to you?
2-• Did you become friends and did your friendship last long?
1-• Were you glad you attempted to talk to them?

The beginning and ending sentences come from the initial paragraph, and many students like to begin like this: "If I . . . ." or "The person that I met was . . . ." This is perfectly acceptable; however, I wanted them to write a spiced-up beginning by concentrating on the main idea of the initial paragraph, which was meeting a particular person. This is how I taught beginnings: we started with the person's name, made it a compound sentence, and ended with a figurative language expression.

Judith Kristen-West was the individual I wanted to meet once, and having the opportunity to make her acquaintance was simply a walk in the park. She transferred to our school in November and she didn't know anyone.

Judith was really cute, very smart, and, at first, kind of quiet. It was a fact that she sat next to me, but I felt the opportunity to talk to her was just around the corner. One morning Judith dropped her pencil, and it rolled right up to my foot. This was my chance, and I seized the moment.

I picked it up, and said, "Excuse me! Is this your pencil?" She took it and blushed. Boy was I excited, and now that the ice was broken, I found out that she was beautiful both inside and out.

Judith and I became friends instantly, and to this day she is helpful, friendly, and always willing to talk to me. She has many other meaningful friends now and has become one of the most well-liked kids in school today.

I was very happy that Judith became my friend because she turned out to be a gem of a friend, and sometimes meeting a new student is not a piece of cake.

Perhaps meeting new people may be difficult, but that day I literally found out what goes around comes around, and now she is a friend for life.

There are several spicy sentences and concepts used in this poem prompt: a beginning sentence, compound sentences, listing sentences, fact/opinion, figurative language, and a direct quote to name a few. Notice how it is almost written like an expository because it is basically a true story. Just write the spice acronyms on the planning page, find the number of questions asked in each bullet, and begin. Always initiate the answer with a spicy beginning, a risky middle, and end it with some kind of unusual twist. This leaves the reader with a completed and full feeling.

34. Open-Ended Questions

Many open-ended questions can be answered using the same technique listed above, provided you use details, explanations, and examples taken from the selection read. Questions used in open-ended areas usually want to know how the student compares to, differs from, feels, or thinks about a certain situation because as long as you give a complete, comprehensive response, there is no wrong answer. The explanation is the key, and using spice helps with its delivery.

If you could ask a famous person, alive or deceased, several questions, what would they be, and why are they worthy questions?

- What are your questions?
- Why are they worthy questions?

There are approximately six answers to this question, and finding them is the trick. Once a question asks for at least three reasons, ideas, thoughts, or anything, it opens the door for a transitional response. This kind of answer is organized, complete, and easy to read. Use the spice acronym from Chapter 29 and begin your response. An example of a skeleton response appears below.

Martin L. King is one of the most admired and respected men of all time, and the questions I would ask him would be worth their weight in gold. As he is one of my heroes, it would be easy for me to talk to him.

First, I would like to know _____? This is a worthy question because _____(listing), _____ and _____.

Next, was it _____? This question is important because it was a fact that _____(fact/opinion), but in my opinion, _____.

Finally, were you hopeful and helpful when you _____(compound question) _____, or did _____? The worthiness of this question is _____(compound answer) _____ because _____ and _____.

Perhaps Dr. King might think my questions are _____, but I'd like him to know that when the going got tough, he got going.

If an open-ended question did not require three answers, we would just add spice where needed and complete it accordingly.

Many times I taught my students to give more details than needed in order to have all the bases covered and to give Jack a thorough and completed answer.

35. Expository Writing

Expositories are another form of writing prompt that simply explains real life situations that occur during actual experiences. Re-telling a story can be done in a couple of ways. Transitional stories put events in order, and for younger students, this is usually very helpful. For older students, writing a "true narrative" or explaining the story is also generally correct, and its explanation can be written in a simple essay. Using spice brings it to life, and using dialogue more often will explain how characters interact in various situations throughout the article.

Just keep the essay as realistic as possible and elaborate on events that occurred during the experience being written about. Possible topics include a trip to the museum, learning how to play baseball, going to the store, my first baseball game, and, of course, what I did last summer.

VI. Timing Standard

36. Drilling for Timed Tests

Many standardized tests are timed, and I feel this is the only part that is truly "teaching to a test". If we are in a race, then we have to teach a race.

In the beginning stages of writing, timing takes a back seat, but as the year progresses, timing begins to come into play. Start by timing single sentences, but be lenient at first. An example of a timed assignment appears below.

> *Write a compound sentence about something you enjoy doing. You have exactly one minute.*

This activity keeps children on task, and it usually works. Throw out hints if needed and give as much encouragement as possible to slower learners. Keep repeating this procedure with various kinds of spice until you feel their writing begins to flow easily.

Timing a story or essay must be introduced slowly in the beginning because it puts pressure on the students and sometimes inhibits the thinking process. Being rushed causes many students to make careless mistakes and can interfere with the final proofreading of a written assignment.

Many stories are only allotted twenty-five minutes, and this also includes the necessary planning. For this kind of story, you need to start by actually doing an entire story and web with the students in about an hour. You have to do the pacing and keep the children on task. The next story is completed individually and given about an hour so that the time factor starts to come into play. The third story is handled by having the kids do a web, untimed, and then forty-five minutes for writing the selection. The fourth story is also given forty-five minutes; however, this also includes the web. The general rule is five minutes for planning and twenty minutes for writing, but I feel twenty minutes puts too much pressure on students, especially when proofreading is a must.

After allowing forty-five minutes for the planning and the story, timing should become a daily factor. The goal is a twenty-five minute target.

This is where you have to start shortening the planning section and giving more time for story writing. Planning is important, but the story or essay is what is graded. By this time the student has a firm grip on spice, sequence, and ideas, planning becomes a simple task. Try to keep the planning to two or three minutes so you have twenty-two or twenty-three minutes for writing and proofreading. The next story is given forty minutes as we try to get closer to our twenty-five minute goal. The sixth story gets thirty-five minutes, the seventh story is thirty minutes, and by the eighth story, we are at our twenty-five minute mark. By this time, your students are ready, and it only took eight stories. It is probably around January, and you have two months to polish up and proceed to the advanced proficient range for many of your enriched students.

As the test time nears, planning can be as simple as a main idea, a short sequence of events, and the spice acronym used for a varied sentence structure check-off list.

Example: A trip to the city's historical museum

I	
B	Got there
A	Walked around
E	Got lost
A	Had fun
L	Saw many things
C	Learned a lot
F	Saw a show

F	Went shopping
T	Came home
D	Told parents
H	Reflected on day
R	
A	

The web took about one minute to plan, and it gives the child twenty-four minutes to complete their story and, ideally, to proofread it.

For forty-five minute timed selections, follow the same procedure, but increase the initial time frame.

Many times, a persuasive essay has a forty-five minute limit. It comes down to a five-minute planning period and eight minutes per paragraph for proofreading purposes. Many times you can break these paragraphs down to smaller time frames for extra timing drill, for example:

> *First, write one five-sentence paragraph in eight minutes. Next, write two paragraphs in sixteen minutes, and so on. This helps with each separate paragraph and timing becomes a little less stressful when required to write five paragraphs in forty minutes.*

This is a sample persuasive web that took minimal time to complete.

Topic: School Six Months a Year

	positive	negative
I		
B	1. More free time	1. Bored?
A	2. More fun time	2. Miss a lot of friends
E	3. More friend time	3. Miss new experiences
A		4. Learn less
L		5. Less prepared for college
C		6. Miss sports in school
F		7. Dr. Jones
F		8. Statistics
T		
D		
H		
R		
A		

Since these tests are timed, teachers have to tackle this concept for many children. Special education students may be exempt from timing restrictions, so they should let their students plan and write at their own speed. This is when detailed planning and slow-paced writing can actually bring their writing level up to a proficient level.

VII. Encouragement

37. Motivational Techniques

Motivating students to give their best is a technique that requires the teacher to act like an entertainer. Being in the same situation all year long seems to breed complacency, and the motivating factor tends to get lost at times. This is commonplace in many schools and not an easy thing to turn around. Come test time, however, motivation becomes necessary, and the teacher, principal, support staff, and students need to take an active role in order to make it happen. The school administration needs to have pep rallies, bring in motivational speakers, and make a big deal about these tests so that the children take them seriously.

About a week prior to test is a good time to begin the hype. Each teacher needs to do anything that works to motivate every student in his or her class. Individual talks sometimes work wonders because you know each student's work habits. With younger children, motivation is easier because they enjoy simple things, but after sixth grade, it becomes increasingly more difficult. This is one reason I admire middle school teachers and feel their job is more challenging. I used coupons marked like hundred dollar bills for younger children up to fifth grade. I'd tell my students that if I noticed a sincere effort during test time, I would pay them $500. They could trade this money in for various prizes, like homework passes or computer time. I'd also tell them no homework that week, even though homework was not given during test time. I'd also take them out for recess for one hour after the test every day. Use any possible motivational techniques necessary because the children need to be at the top of their game on those days.

For older students, have pizza parties, concerts, a dance, treats at lunch, and homework passes. Just remember to make sure they give their best because to many, it's just another test, and by this time they have already been tested-out.

Motivation for high school students is easy because if they don't pass the test, they don't graduate; however, many middle school students need to be pushed because of their age level and lukewarm tendencies to give their best during this time of year.

VIII. The Right Direction

38. Cross Content Connection

Spelling is a necessary part of all subjects but should parallel the instruction of the week. This is a must in order to have universal subject related vocabulary needed for understanding and teaching.

For younger children it usually has to take the traditional approach, but as the level of skills increase so does the spelling list.

Making up your own list of spelling words is an extremely effective way to match your words with skills and lessons taught. As important as spelling is, teachers can control this discipline and use it to their advantage. In self-contained classrooms spelling words from all subjects can be incorporated into a single spelling unit. This enables teachers to use one test for multiple grades in various subjects.

Cross-teaching with spelling is extremely easy because you can have words from different subjects and use them in many different ways. Your spelling list can be as diverse as you wish because you are the creator. Here is an example of a spelling unit for grades 2 through 8. Please notice definitions are given with examples or pictures in order to make the meaning easier to understand, apply, and remember.

Lesson 1 – (Math, Language, Reading, Science, and Social Studies)

1. Digit (1-4-7) any single number
2. Numeral (7-56-726) any number
3. Area ("A" two times which means "A" squared or "A^2")

A

A | **Area means the space inside of a shape**

4. Perimeter – pe (rim) i (t) er – plus the rim
5. Theme – The Boy Who Cried Wolf (DON'T LIE!!!)
6. Figurative language – piece of cake, easy as one, two, three
7. Gravity – down force, "Ouch, I fell!!"
8. Revolution – Duck, duck, goose/walk around the school
9. Rotation – a spinning top, getting dizzy
10. Predicting outcome – what's next?
11. Vertices – more than one angle
12. Equator – my belt

Many students also like a challenge word so always try to include some kind of big or grownup word. Example: semi-darkness, hypotheses, or literally. Using big words shows power and command of the language, but don't use it too much.

Various upper-grade spelling or vocabulary lists may include: prefix lists, figurative language lists, math word lists, compound or complex sentences list, transitional word lists.

These skills are tested by writing sentences or short stories including each skill. This is an application test and shows correct usage, not just spellings and definitions. It is very useful.

Examples of cross-teaching sentences:

> *The <u>gravity</u> of the situation was apparent, but John knew he could handle the pressure.*
>
> *This <u>area</u> seems to be covered with a thick <u>emotional</u> <u>atmosphere</u>, but was handled as easy as pie using <u>level-headed</u> actions.*

In the ever-changing world of education, teachers need to find ways to cross-teach and spelling in a definite way to begin this approach.

IX. Conclusion

39. Summation

Many of the strategies mentioned in this book have come about by the ever-changing world of writing testing. As a teacher, I found that teaching children how to write was an extremely challenging task, but using these methods made it possible. I never thought of writing a book or becoming a consultant, but I became so confident that my techniques worked that they gave me the encouragement and motivation to share these strategies with other educators from kindergarten to college. After twenty-eight and a half years of teaching writing, I've come to realize that if you teach a child how to write, then bending the writing to any prompt, essay, or paper is a lot easier than teaching to a test. The skill of writing will always stay with the student and will remain a lifelong asset.

In closing, just remember these words: Old teachers never die, they just lose their class.

Your students will remember you as a person forever, but if they're going to remember anything at all about you - "The Teacher" - let them remember that you were the one who taught them how to write.

SPICE
Up
YOUR WRITING

SPICE IT UP

APPENDIX

Writing with SPICE

☆☆☆   ☆☆☆

FIGURATIVE LANGUAGE PHRASES

At the drop of a hat
Back to square one
Bed of roses
Burn the midnight oil
Butterfingers
Coast clear
Cold feet
Down in the dumps
Ears are burning
Easy as cake
Final straw
Forty winks
Give me a hand
In a nutshell
In a pickle
In the bag
It was like magic
It's all Greek to me
Let the cat out of the bag
Long shot
Mum's the word
On the ball
Out on a limb

Pass the buck
Pay through the nose
Read between the lines
Saved by the bell
Spill the beans
Take a rain check
Under the weather
Up my sleeve
World on my shoulders

<u>Work Sheet</u>   <u>Give an Example of Each</u>

<u>Figurative Language</u>   <u>Beginning Sentence</u>

<u>Compound Sentences = 2 sentences with
GLUE (and, but, or)</u>

<u>Use alliteration in your title!</u>   <u>INDENT</u>

<u>Fact/Opinion</u>   <u>Use descriptive words = adjectives!</u>

<u>Listing Sentences</u>   <u>Use transitional words</u>

<u>Prefixes / Suffixes</u>

<u>Dialogue – Use ONCE in writing!</u>   <u>Ending Sentence</u>

Don't forget to indent!

1. <u>Beginning Sentences</u>
    Last week
    About three days ago
    Many years ago

2. <u>Ending Sentences</u>
    At last
    Perhaps
    It almost
    Once Again

3. <u>Use descriptive words = adjectives!</u>
    I like to eat gooey, warm brownies and steaming hot apple pie.

4. <u>Compound Sentences = 2 sentences with GLUE (and, but, or)</u>
    I like cake, and I like ice cream.
    A better sentence: I like warm chocolate cake, and I like ice cream sundaes.

5. <u>Listing Sentences</u>
    I like cake, ice cream, and soda.
    A better sentence: I like warm chocolate cake, ice cream sundaes, and a freezing mug of ice cold root beer. (ADD descriptive words!)

6. <u>Figurative Language</u>

Give me a hand	Easy as pie
Not a piece of cake	24/7
Over the hill	On cloud nine
A piece of cake	Raining cats and dogs
Skating on thin ice	

7. <u>Fact/Opinion</u>

It is a fact that the Eagles did not win many games this season, but in my opinion I think they played very well.

8. <u>Prefixes/Suffixes</u>

Rewrite
Careless
Semidarkness

9. <u>Use Alliteration in your Title!</u>

McNabb's Magical Moment
Danny Drives Dangerously

10. <u>Dialogue – Use ONCE in writing!</u>

Bob said, "Thanks for the present!"
Susan asked, "Can you come over today?"
Kevin replied, "I'll ask my mom."

11. <u>Use transition words</u>

First, Next, Then, Last

Letter Clue	Word Clue	Meaning
I	I	Indent – Use two fingers
B	Begin	Beginning – Last week, about three days ago, many years ago, there once was, last night/week/month/year
A	And	Affixes – Prefixes and suffixes on some words
E	End	Ending – At last, perhaps, it almost, once again
A	All	Apostrophes – 's or s' (possessives)
L	Long	Listing – Using commas in a list
C	Compositions	Compound words, subjects, predicates, sentences
F	For	Figurative language – Piece of cake, easy as pie, over the hill, raining cats and dogs, on cloud nine, skating on thin ice
F	Fantastic	Fact/Opinion – It is a fact that . . . , but in my opinion . . . .
T	Teachers	Transitional words – First, next, lastly
D	Down	Direct quotation – Include 1
H	Here	Homophones
R	Right	Rhetorical question – Include 1
A	Away	Anything else

I Begin And End All Long Compositions For Fantastic Teachers Down Here Right Away.

Titles – Use alliteration:

Casey's Courageous Comeback
Sally's Silly Solution
Paul's Pitiful Play

Tips for Good Writing

When you begin to write, you may want to use one of the following beginnings:

Many...   In a land far away...
Many years ago...   (Someone's name) was...
A few...   On July 2, 1993...
There once was...   About three days,
weeks...   Years ago...
Last night...week...month...year   Once...

When you are ready to end your story you may want to use one of the following endings:

Finally...
At last...
Once again...
Years...Days...Months...Weeks...Later
Near the end...
It almost...
The...
Perhaps...
Maybe...
Although...

WRITER'S CHECKLIST

Did you remember to . . .

- ✓ Keep the central idea or topic in mind?
- ✓ Keep your audience in mind?
- ✓ Support your ideas with details, explanations, and examples?
- ✓ State your ideas in a clear sequence?
- ✓ Include an opening and a closing?
- ✓ Use a variety of words and vary your sentence structure?
- ✓ State your opinion or conclusion clearly?
- ✓ Capitalize, spell, and use punctuation correctly?
- ✓ Write neatly? / Print or cursive? / Quickly and neatly?

After you write your story, read what you have written. Use the checklist to make certain that your writing is the best it can be.

	Name:_____ *Check off the box, if you've completed the skill*
	Compound Sentences
	Listing Sentences
	Figurative Language
	Direct Quotes
	Varied Sentences
	Words showing possession
	Transition Words
	Fact and Opinion

	Name:_____ *Check off the box, if you've completed the skill*
	Compound Sentences
	Listing Sentences
	Figurative Language
	Direct Quotes
	Varied Sentences
	Words showing possession
	Transition Words
	Fact and Opinion

The Spices of Writing

MEAT	BEGINNING	Start your story with a good beginning using words such as: A few..., Many years..., There once was..., Years ago..., or a quote.
POTATOES	ENDING	When you are ready to end your story you may want to use: Finally..., At last..., Once again..., Perhaps..., It almost..., or another transitional word.
SALT	COMPOUND SENTENCE	Add a compound sentence, compound subject, or a compound predicate in your sentence.
PEPPER	LISTING SENTENCE	Use a listing sentence and remember to use the commas. Ex. The moist grass, dark soil, and bright sun made it the perfect environment for the plants to grow.
GARLIC	FIGURATIVE LANGUAGE	Spice up your writing with figurative language. This is as easy as pie to use in your writing. This shows that you are on the ball.
CHILI POWDER and PARSLEY	PREFIXES AND SUFFIXES	Rearrange your sentences so that you have refreshing words using prefixes and suffixes. Be unafraid to take a chance. This is painless to do.
Don't use too many of one spice. WHY?	It will not taste delightful, and the reader will not enjoy their meal.	Also, remember our pledge to always indent a paragraph. So are you ready to get cooking, now that I have spilled the beans on what it takes to be a good writer?

Teacher-Student Writing Conference

Name:_____ Date _____ Score: _____

_____

Keepers	Fixers

Who, What, When, Where, Why, How, Because

W, W, W, W, W, H, B

Title

1.

2.

3.

4.

5.

6.

7.

8.

Topic

What Spice will you add?
Direct Quotes
Listing Sentences
Compound words/sentences/
               subjects/predicates
Fact/Opinion
Figurative Language
Transitional Words
Idioms
BIG WORDS
Affixes

Tips for Good Writing: Beginnings and Closings

- When students begin and end prompt writing, it is helpful to have a "bank" of openings to choose from.
- These openings/closings should be modeled by the teacher, and the students (especially students that have trouble coming up with ones on their own) should be able to recall these easily and almost by habit.
- Although the Better Answers Formula is helpful when beginning open-ended reading comprehension questions, these types of beginnings are much more effective when responding to picture prompts, poem prompts, and the new speculative prompt.
- Teach openings/closings with compound sentences and figurative language when students are ready.
- The following sample openings and closings have yielded positive results when included in student responses.

Sample Openings:

- ✓ Many…
- ✓ Many years ago…
- ✓ A few…
- ✓ There once was…
- ✓ Once…
- ✓ Years ago…
- ✓ Last night…week…month…year
- ✓ In a land far away…
- ✓ (Someone's name) was…
- ✓ On (specific date)…
- ✓ About three days…weeks…months…years…

Sample Closings:

- ✓ Finally…
- ✓ At last…
- ✓ Once again…
- ✓ Years…Days…Months…Weeks…Later
- ✓ Near the end…
- ✓ It almost…
- ✓ The…
- ✓ Perhaps…
- ✓ Although…
- ✓ Maybe…

Special thanks to my wife Diane, my brother Steve, my sister Susanne, Jay Dugan, Joann Weigelt, Judith Kristen, and Andrew West for making this book a reality.

Mike Devono spent over a quarter of a century as a teacher in the Garden State. Currently he is a top consultant for the Educational Information & Resource Center (EIRC) in Sewell, NJ. Mike lives with his wife Diane, and their fifteen-year-old year son, Michael in Vineland, New Jersey. The Devono clan completes itself with two darling daschunds named Maxie and DJ. Mike is also a huge football fan and is an NFL Chain Crew Official for the Philadelphia Eagles.